That Cat Max

by Liza Charlesworth
illustrated by Stephen Lewis

SCHOLASTIC INC.
New York • Toronto • London • Auckland • Sydney
Mexico City • New Delhi • Hong Kong • Buenos Aires

Designed by Maria Lilja
ISBN-13: 978-0-439-88451-8 • ISBN-10: 0-439-88451-9
Copyright © 2006 by Scholastic Inc.
All rights reserved. Printed in the U.S.A.

First printing, September 2006

12 11 10 9   9 10 11/0

Phonics Fact

The letter *a* is a vowel. A vowel can make a short sound. The short-*a* sound is found in words such as **that**, **cat**, and **Max**. What other short-*a* words can you find in this story? Look at the pictures, too!

I **am** a **fan** of **that cat Max**. Why?

Max can play catch.

Daffodils

Pansies

Max can cut the **grass**.

Max can chat with **Sandy Blat** about her **brand**-new **tan hat**.

Max can do **crafts**. He made **that fancy basket**.

Max can do **math**! He **adds and subtracts** super **fast**!

Max can cook **ham and mashed yams** in a little **black pan**.

Max can drive the **van** to the **snack stand**.
The **apple** pie there is **grand**!

Max has talent! He **can tap and rap.**

Max can also play **sax** in my **dad's jazz band**.

Max can even **act** like **an acrobat**!

But the best thing **Max can** do…

. . . is **nap** on my **lap**. **Man,** I love **that cat Max!**

Short-a Riddles

Listen to the riddles. Then match each riddle with the right short-*a* word from the box.

> **Word Box**
>
> | fast | grass | cat | tap | jam |
> |------|---------|-----|-----|----------|
> | nap | acrobat | hat | can | subtract |

1 This pet says, "Meow!"

2 It is the opposite of *slow*.

3 This is a lot like jelly.

4 It is the opposite of *can't*.

5 Sleepy babies do this in a crib.

6 You put this on your head to keep warm.

7 It is green and grows in backyards.

8 A person who does gymnastics is called this.

9 It is the opposite of *add*.

10 A kind of dancing that makes a lot of noise.

Short-a Cheer

Hooray for short *a*, the best sound around!

Let's holler short-*a* words all over town!

There's **map** and **plant** and **rap** and **cat**.

There's **pan** and **band** and **stamp** and **hat**.

There's **man** and **grass** and **jazz** and **tap**.

There's **act** and **fast** and **snap** and **clap**.

Short *a*, short *a*, give a great cheer,

For the **happiest** sound that you ever will hear!

Make a list of other short-*a* words. Then use them in your cheer.